LESSONS FROM THE GLOBAL FINANCIAL CRISIS

*The relevance
of Adam Smith on morality
and free markets*

T0040044

RICHARD MORGAN

Taylor Trade Publishing

A Connor Court Book

Lanham • Boulder • New York • Toronto • Plymouth, UK

Published by Taylor Trade Publishing
An imprint of The Rowman & Littlefield Publishing Group, Inc.
4501 Forbes Boulevard, Suite 200, Lanham, Maryland 20706
http://www.rlpgtrade.com

Estover Road, Plymouth PL6 7PY, United Kingdom

Distributed by National Book Network

British Library Cataloguing in Publication Information Available

Library of Congress Cataloging-in-Publication Data Available

ISBN 978-1-58979-577-8 (pbk. : alk. paper)

♾™ The paper used in this publication meets the minimum requirements of
American National Standard for Information Sciences—Permanence of Paper
for Printed Library Materials, ANSI/NISO Z39.48-1992.

Printed in the United States of America

"Wherein consisted the happiness and perfection of a man, considered not only as an individual, but as the member of a family, of a state, and of the great society of mankind, was the object which the ancient moral philosophy proposed to investigate...

In the ancient philosophy the perfection of virtue was represented as necessarily productive, to the person who possessed it, of the most perfect happiness in this life."

The Wealth of Nations

ACKNOWLEDGEMENTS

Although the views expressed are the responsibility of the writer, I am grateful for a number of friends and colleagues who have provided invaluable assistance in the preparation of this work. I particularly mention Jim Donaldson, Ian McFarling and Graham Sellars-Jones, who have helped on a more or less regular basis. Others who were generous with their time and contribution include John Kiely, Ian McDonald, Des Moore, Andrew Shearer and Tim Tyler.

CONTENTS

PREFACE

The global financial crisis has challenged the belief that free markets are the best way of organising economic activity. It has suggested to many that free markets lead to greed and that greed leads to indifference to the well-being of others. An unintended consequence of greed-driven markets is seen to be financial collapse, a collapse that harms all, not just the greedy. This might suggest that the ideas of Adam Smith, a founding thinker and extoller of the benefits of free markets, are no longer relevant. Richard Morgan, in this valuable book, counters this suggestion by presenting a nuanced account of Adam Smith's ideas in which markets are seen as mitigating greed, and in which an important role is seen for limited government regulation of markets.

Morgan emphasises Smith's stress on the importance of virtue for individual behaviour and the idea from ancient philosophy that virtuous behaviour leads to "the most perfect happiness." The incentive of happiness to encourage people to act virtuously is reinforced by the argument of Adam Smith that social interactions, including market interactions, reveal to people the importance of empathy with others and the danger to their self-interest of treating people unfairly. Thus, virtue and self-interest are encouraged by market activity.

In recent years a new area in economics has risen, that is the area of behavioural economics. Morgan sees ideas and empirical findings from behavioural economics as supportive of Smith's views. For example, Morgan points out that Smith's view that benevolence is a part of human nature is supported by the results of controlled experiments in behavioural economics. Here the evidence from the ultimatum game and the dictator game are very compelling. Other ideas from behavioural economics, in particular present bias and self-serving bias, are also shown by Morgan to be supportive of Smith's views.

The global financial crisis would not appear to Smith as unprecedented. Smith was well-aware of financial crises and incorporated their threat into his economic views. Smith observed from financial crises such as the 1772 crisis in Scotland, which, Morgan reports, reduced 30 banks to three, that an unregulated banking system posed great risks for society. Smith's argument for government regulation of banks, as quoted by Morgan, p.38, is based on a negative externality, in that the security offered by the banking system to all people can be endangered by the actions of a few individuals.

Morgan's exposition balances Smith's argument that markets devoid of government regulation can defeat themselves with Smith's scepticism about the wisdom of government decision-makers. In Morgan's view, governments bear some of the responsibility for the GFC in failing to control the amount and type of credit. More generally, Morgan reminds us of Smith's warning to beware of "the man of system", that conceited individual enamoured with his ideal plan of government. The 20th century has chilling examples of catastrophes due to men of system. Less far reaching examples occur regularly in contemporary democracies. Perhaps a weakness of people to believe that a simple answer exists for economic and social problems makes them prey to "man of system" thinking.

Richard Morgan has made a valuable contribution with this book, by bringing together succinctly Adam Smith's work on markets and on morality, that is The Wealth of Nations and The Theory of Moral Sentiments. The importance of the latter is being increasingly recognized by economists at the current time, correcting an excessive focus on the Wealth of Nations in recent decades. Furthermore, bringing into his discussion ideas and evidence from the new field of behavioural economics, Morgan enhances the contemporary relevance of this book. And of course confronting the ideas of Adam Smith with the global financial crisis sets these ideas in the context of a most important practical issue. In my view, this book is both illuminating and stimulating.

Ian M. McDonald.
University of Melbourne.

INTRODUCTION

This work takes into account and includes discussion on recent world economic events and the enduring relevance of Adam Smith's insights as reflected in *The Wealth of Nations.*

A key conclusion remains that free markets continue to be the best path to economic wellbeing notwithstanding periodic downturns.

Accompanying his advocacy of free markets, Smith believed in strong but limited government. He endorsed the need for a legal system to protect liberty and property rights, national defence, public works and regulations which the community accepts as necessary and that protect the public without abandoning a free market philosophy. These views refute the contention that Smith supported complete laissez-faire economics.

At the time he perceived that specialisation involving repetitive work could have a debilitating effect and advocated universal education to provide for broader employment opportunities. He accepted that government had an important role to play in ensuring a "well governed society."

The notion that free markets encouraged greed and

exploitation is alien to Smith's philosophy. He would have rejected any notion that greed is good, and would have claimed that embracing his ideas would at least minimise greed.

The effect of unbridled greed and moral failure, accompanied by failure of government regulation, have been all too evident in the recent world financial crisis. Confidence has been shaken in free markets and in governments in the developed and the developing world alike.

Importance of Moral Framework

This work challenges the assertion that Adam Smith in any way condoned greed or exploitation. In fact, he was a particular critic of actions which harmed the weak and the poor.

There is an explanation of the key elements of the moral framework he identified, in particular the virtues of prudence and justice, which he saw as relevant to the functioning of a free market economy.

His conclusions are still valid. In the context of today's world financial crisis, however, it is apparent that business and government have strayed from those standards and would have been condemned by Smith. At a time when free market economics is being questioned in some quarters it is therefore timely to focus on the relevance of Smith's economic case for free markets and his moral hilosophy as a guide for government and commerce.

Smith can be said to have been the first thinker to

explain in detail how wealth is created and what really drives modern economies. That was over two hundred years ago in his widely acclaimed treatise, *An Inquiry into the Nature and Causes of The Wealth of Nations* (*The Wealth of Nations*), first published in 1776.

But some twenty five years before that, the lectures he delivered in 1750-51, when he was Professor of Logic at Glasgow University, "contained many of the most important opinions in *The Wealth of Nations*[1] and predated his first major work *The Theory of Moral Sentiments*, published in 1759. He was appointed to the position of Professor of Moral Philosophy at Glasgow University in 1752.

Today, *The Wealth of Nations* is generally considered to be the foundation of the discipline of economics. In the 18th century, however, there was no separate discipline called economics, and Smith spent most of his professional life as Professor of Moral Philosophy considering far more than just the causes of wealth. He published work on astronomy, rhetoric, language and ethics. He did not complete his proposed third major work on jurisprudence and government, but student notes of his lectures have now been published.

Finally, the implications of his moral principles and economic analysis are reviewed in the light of present day circumstances.

For readers not familiar with Adam Smith, there is an Addendum which provides a diagram identifying the key

---

1 Stewart, Dugald, 'Account of the Life and Writings of Adam Smith', 1793, p. 33

elements of his economic analysis, together with relevant quotations selected from the two major publications.

Richard Morgan, AM,

Melbourne, Australia

October 2009

SMITH'S LIFE AND CAREER

Adam Smith was born in Kirkcaldy, Scotland in 1723. His father died a few months before he was born and he was brought up by his mother for whom he always had the greatest of affection.

He went to school in Kirkcaldy before going to Glasgow University in 1737 at the age of fourteen. Smith was an outstanding scholar and was awarded the Snell Exhibition for the best student to go to Balliol College, Oxford University. There is an early account of the "extraordinary powers of his memory" given by Dugald Stewart.[2]

Smith left Scotland for Oxford riding on horseback in 1740, and he remained there without a break for six years. He was critical of the teaching standards and was later to say so in *The Wealth of Nations*. Apparently, the University was not impressed by his comments. Despite becoming one of Oxford's most famous sons, and a leading figure of The Scottish Enlightenment, he received no honour from the University to recognise his achievements.

Smith however made the most of the excellent Balliol

---

2 Stewart, Dugald, 'Account of the Life and Writings of Adam Smith', 1793, p. 33

library, although his reading was restricted by standards of the time; "He was one day detected reading Hume's *Treatise of Human Nature* – probably the very copy presented to him by the author – and was punished by severe reprimand and confiscation of the evil book."[3] His main interest and strength was in ancient Latin and Greek classics.

There were other difficulties. Of the one hundred students, only eight were from Scotland and they "seemed to have been always treated as an alien and intrusive faction."[4]

On returning to Scotland, Smith gave very successful public lectures on English literature, before becoming Professor of Logic at Glasgow University in 1751, and later Professor of Moral Philosophy in 1752, a position he held until 1763.

He left the University to become tutor to the Duke of Buccleugh. They traveled to the Continent meeting leading philosophers, including Voltaire and the physiocrats in France.

On returning to Scotland he lived in Kilkcardy writing *The Wealth of Nations*. "The book took twelve years to write, and was in contemplation for probably twelve years before that." [5]

He concluded his career with an appointment in 1777 to the position of Commissioner of Customs in Scotland.

---

3 Rae, John, 'The Life of Adam Smith', p. 24
4 Rae, John, 'The Life of Adam Smith', p. 26
5 Ibid

Smith, with his health failing in 1790, requested his close friends Dr Joseph Black (the father of chemistry) and Dr James Hutton (the father of geology), both also leading figures of The Scottish Enlightenment, to destroy all his papers, apart from a few selected items, possibly to ensure he was not misquoted from earlier work. He may also have been concerned that controversial views on the role of the Monarchy expressed in correspondence could compromise his friends.

His friends were gathered near the end and when he left their company for the last time, it is reported he said "I believe we must adjourn this meeting to some other place." He died on 17 July 1790, aged 67.

THE PHILOSOPHER ECONOMIST

Smith's methods of enquiry reflected those of Sir Isaac Newton (1642 – 1727), whom he admired as one of the great scientists of all time. Newton's understanding of gravity, for example, enabled him to provide a comprehensive explanation of the solar system which had eluded earlier scholars. Newton was an empiricist whose work was based on observation and testing theories against observed facts.

Smith used the empirical method to study observations and look for systems which explained human behavior.

In the first instance, he explained social cohesion in his early major work, *The Theory of Moral Sentiments*, and he then went on in this work to consider ethical principles. In respect to the latter, he was influenced by the four classic or cardinal virtues as follows:

- Temperance – moderation in everything said and done.
- Courage – is displayed in toils and dangers.
- Prudence – caution and discretion in bettering our condition.

- Justice – rendering to every man his due and with faithful discharge of obligations assured.

Smith included the display of self-command as a virtue, which he saw guiding the moral propriety of action in respect of the other virtues and therefore moral autonomy.

The four virtues particularly associated with Smith are prudence, justice, beneficence and self-command. For him, prudence and justice provided the most important link between free markets and virtue.

Smith was influenced by Cicero and other classic authors.[6] Cicero refers to the classic virtues as "perception of truth... preserving a fellowship among men, with assigning to each his own" and again "all that is morally right rises from some or one of four sources (virtues)."[7]

The influence of the classic virtues has come down to us through the teaching of Christianity, which absorbed much of ancient philosophy through the work of St. Thomas Aquinas, who stated "a cardinal virtue is concerned with the main points in human life; like a hinge on which a door turns."[8]

Today, the Catholic Church has recognised virtue in business. Pope John Paul II's 1991 social encyclical, as summarised by Dr Samuel Gregg, moral theologian formerly with The Centre for Independent Studies, "stressed the virtuous nature of entrepreneurial

---

6 See p. 32
7 Cicero, 'On Duties', p. 17
8 Montes, Leonidas, 'Adam Smith in Context', p. 57

activity, praised business and the market economy and recommended the free economy as a model for the former Communist and Third World nations." Virtue in business is not however universally recognised by other Churches.

Smith evidently also had the virtues very much in mind in his second major work *The Wealth of Nations*, when he said "In the ancient philosophy the perfection of virtue was represented as necessarily productive, to the person who possessed it, of the most perfect happiness in this life."[9]

In many respects, the two publications, *The Theory of Moral Sentiments* and *The Wealth of Nations*, can be treated and read as two parts of one work and this is the view taken by this writer. Reviewing Smith's moral and economic insights together emphasises what John Maynard Keynes had to say in writing to Roy Harrod in 1938: "I want to emphasise strongly the point about economics being a moral science."[10]

---

9 Adam Smith, 'The Wealth of Nations' (WN) B.V, ch.1, V.1.158
10 Montes, Leonidas , 'Adam Smith in Context', p. 144

SMITH AND SOCIAL COHESION

At first, however, we need to follow the outline of his observations in *The Theory of Moral Sentiments* concerning social interaction and ethics. His insights have universal relevance, including to the conduct of commerce.

During social interaction, which would include meeting for the purpose of exchanging goods, Smith observed the faculty of empathy (which he called sympathy) and how it enables people to empathise with others and gauge how they are reacting to the behavior of the observer and whether their response is agreeable or disagreeable.

As humans generally prefer approbation to disapprobation they are quick to adjust their behavior to achieve approbation or at least avoid disapprobation. Although not intended, the process which he refers to as "the hidden hand" provides for adjustments to behavior which favour social cohesion.

Like gravity, the elements at work are invisible and we can only observe the effects. He assigns the design of the system governing society as the working of a higher being or God, but his work or interest did not extend far into the subject of theology.

Smith makes a number of observations to support his conclusion about the faculty of empathy. For example, "the mob, when they are gazing at a dancer on the slack rope, naturally writhe and twist and balance their own bodies, as they see him do, and as they feel that they themselves must do if in his situation."[11]

He makes it clear his reference to sympathy is not limited to pity and compassion. He says "sympathy, though its meaning was, perhaps, originally the same, may now, however, without much impropriety, be made use of to denote our fellow feeling with any passion whatever."[12]

---

11 'The Theory of Moral Sentiments' (TMS), part I, section I, ch. I.I.3
12 TMS part I, section I, ch. I.I.5

MORAL JUDGMENTS

Smith saw the process of social adjustment also providing for moral judgment of ones self and others with the guidance of what he called the 'impartial spectator' – that is the man within oneself as it were, and therefore the ability to judge from the perspective of a disinterested third party. This is an observation consistent with the Platonic metaphor of the chariot driver and the black horse and white horse. The black horse stands for bad, and the white for good, and the chariot driver (Smith's impartial spectator) is in command, making moral judgments of oneself and others. These three elements of the mind were later classified by Freud as ego, id and super ego.

For Smith, self-command held particular importance. He saw self-command as the principal agent governing the propriety of action in respect of the other virtues, and for this reason he stressed the importance of early training in the habits of self-command. He quite rightly, and perhaps a little wryly (he never married), observed babies are not born with any sense of self-command and the need for training is all too evident.

He says the principles of self-command are "upon most

occasions, principally and almost entirely recommended to us by one; by the sense of propriety, by regard to the sentiments of the supposed impartial spectator. Without the restraint which this principle imposes, every passion would, upon most occasions, rush headlong, if I may say so, to its own gratification."[13]

In terms to which we can easily relate, the impartial spectator is the voice within that tells us not to have that extra chocolate, testing the virtue of temperance! Our level of self-command then determines how we act.

---

13 TMS, part VI, section I, ch. VI.III.55

HOW LIVING STANDARDS ARE IMPROVED

S mith's following major work *The Wealth of Nations* provided an analysis of how the very characteristics of the free market system are likely to produce the best results in terms of improved living standards.

He stressed it was not, as the mercantilists believed, that reserves of gold and silver determined national wealth, but the quantity of goods and services produced.

The following graph shows how per capita incomes rose in England, despite the impact of wars and the depression, after the publication of *The Wealth of Nations* and the freeing up of trade and markets.[14]

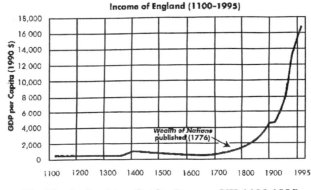

The Rise in Real per Capita Income, UK 1100-1995

---

14 Skousen, Mark, 'The Making of Modern Economics', p. 15

Smith particularly stressed that the living standards for the poor were improved with free markets and his expectations have been confirmed.

A World Bank report published in September 2008 stated "poverty has been declining at the rate of about one percentage point a year from 52% of the developing world's population in 1981 to 25% in 2005. This is no small achievement, given that the number of poor fell by five hundred million in this period." This all occurred during a period of freeing up of world markets.

It is often held under free markets that the rich get richer and the poor get poorer. However the results of a US survey refute this perception as indicated by the following:

U.S. Living Standards, 1900 - 1970[15]

Percentage of Households With: %	Among All Families in 1900 %	Among Poor Families in 1970 %
Flush toilets	15	99
Running water	24	92
Central heating	1	58
One (or fewer) occupants per room	48	96
Electricity	3	99
Refrigeration	18	99
Automobiles	1	41

Smith observed two aspects of human nature that, together, provided an incentive for specialisation which he saw as the major contributor to increased labour productivity and wealth creation. The first of his insights

15 Skousen, Mark, 'The Making of Modern Economics', p. 26

was the "propensity to truck, barter and exchange one thing for another."[16] Second was the instinct of self-preservation and bettering one's condition.

He saw that from earliest times mankind was quick to appreciate that one's condition could be improved by specialising in a trade or craft and exchanging goods. Later, money provided the means of moving away from barter to a broader opportunity for exchange, money being the intermediary.

Finally, capital, innovation and freeing up of markets enhanced the opportunity for specialisation to contribute to further labour productivity and improve living standards.

That specialisation is required for productivity improvement is a feature in any political economy and is not peculiar to capitalism. But Smith saw wealth creation in the free market economy as providing the resources for education and a higher standard of living to overcome what he perceived at the time as the negative impact of repetitive work.

Reflecting his concern about the effects which can flow from increasing specialisation, he judged education should not be left to the market alone, and the State should ensure universal education to provide for broader employment opportunities.

This was a proposal that showed he believed the State should ensure essential community requirements not fully met by the free market - a point not generally appreciated by his critics.

---

16 WN, B.I, ch.2, I.2.1

SMITH AND SELF INTEREST

Despite his conclusions about the benefits of a free market, with an appropriate role for the State, critics have denigrated the free market economy and Smith's advocacy of that system. The system is perceived by its critics to be based on selfishness or, in 1829 by its critics in France, "... exploitation, in the sense of turning to account for selfish purposes."[17]

For today's critics, the term selfishness has been replaced by reference to greed and, if that is not sufficiently colourful, "crass greed." "Greed is good" is even said to be the creed of the proponents of free markets and in today's universal media this has gained widespread publicity. Such negative perceptions of the market economy have the potential to undermine its moral foundation and therefore its general acceptance.

In today's economic climate this has been further highlighted by the current debate in a number of countries over executive remuneration packages, and in particular with companies experiencing a profit down-turn or financial difficulties. Smith recognised the potential for such behaviour with joint stock companies because the interests of those in control were not

---

17 Coleman, Dr. William, 'Economics and its Enemies', p.137

necessarily aligned with the owners of capital.

There is a long history of the perception that we are by nature selfish. Amongst its proponents are Thomas Hobbes, Karl Marx (in respect of capitalism generally and against the owners of capital in particular) and more recently people such as the novelist and philosopher, Iris Murdoch. Such a perception of human nature supports the case for more State control of the lives of its citizens, in order to limit their perceived selfishness.

Their view is at odds with Smith on two counts. First, the part benevolence plays in community life needs to be weighed against claims that people are by nature solely guided by selfish motives. He observed benevolence is part of human nature and mentions how often we see love and compassion particularly within the family and communities in times of stress. He commended the virtue of beneficence. Second, his understanding of self-interest was quite different from selfishness or greed, as discussed in the following chapter.

THE IMPORTANCE OF
BENEVOLENCE

Smith saw benevolence as part of human nature. He said "How selfish soever man may be supposed, there are evidently some principles in his nature, which interest him in the fortune of others, and render their happiness necessary to him, though he derives nothing from it except the pleasure of seeing it."[18]

Of the virtue of beneficence he goes on to say; "And hence it is, that to feel much for others and little for ourselves, that to restrain our selfish, and to indulge our benevolent affections, constitutes the perfection of human nature..."[19]

It would seem all too obvious that many actions are benevolent and not selfish. Year after year numerous exceptional examples are recognised with Bravery Awards.

Take for example, the twelve year old boy in northern Australia whose younger sister was taken by a crocodile. Determined to save her, he jumped on the back of the crocodile which then released his sister. He then dragged

18 TMS, part I, section I, ch. I.I.44
19 Ibid

her to safety and called the Royal Flying Doctor Service, whose staff were then able to attend to her injuries and ensure a safe recovery.

Recent findings within the discipline of Behavioral Economics have demonstrated a preference for fairness to be innate and strengthen the conclusion that we are not solely guided by selfish motives. Controlled experiments conducted many thousands of times worldwide have shown a consistent finding that most people prefer a fair outcome over a result of taking advantage of the other.[20]

Participants in these experiments seeking unfair outcomes are the exception rather than the rule. They are constrained in a market economy by the need for the buyer and the seller only proceeding with a transaction if it were to their mutual advantage. It is the fear of losing customers, Smith said, "which restrains his frauds and corrects his negligence."[21]

The generation of wealth in a free market economy also provides an opportunity for expression of benevolence, an opportunity that is frequently and consistently taken. For example, the not-for-profit sector of the Australian economy makes a significant contribution to the welfare of the community. Benevolence provides a strong motivation for this sector. The Australian Bureau of Statistics most recent publication showed more than 5.4 million Australians donate more than 700 million hours annually.

---

20 Fehr, Ernst, Gächter, Simon, *The Journal of Economic Perspectives*, vol.14, p. 159
21 WN vol 1, b.I, ch. 10, I.10.86

Benevolence transcends nationality. Globally, not-for-profit organisations make outstanding contributions to the welfare of people in need through voluntary work. For example, The International Federation of Red Cross and Red Crescent Societies have 97 million volunteers worldwide.

The foregoing observations contradict the notion that we are inherently selfish by nature, or as Iris Murdoch claims, that "we are largely mechanical creatures, the slaves of relentlessly strong selfish forces." [22] This implies people are not deserving of, or accountable for, moral autonomy. It is an assertion destructive of self-esteem, an outcome which seems inconsistent with Murdoch's call for love and compassion.

---

22 Murdoch, Iris, 'The Sovereignty of Good Over Other Concepts', p. 381

SELF INTEREST DOES NOT MEAN SELFISH

It is evident that Smith's central notion of self-interest – often misinterpreted by his critics - is quite different from greed or "relentlessly strong selfish forces."

In his first major work, *The Theory of Moral Sentiments*, Smith made it clear he draws on the Stoic notion of self-interest (which he also refers to as synonymous with self-love) which is quite different from selfishness or crass greed. He said, "Every man, as the Stoics used to say, is first and principally recommended to his own care...."[23]

He goes on, "Regard to our own private happiness and interest, too, appear upon many occasions very laudable principles of action. The habits of economy, industry, discretion, attention and application of thought are generally supposed to be cultivated from self-interested motives, and, at the same time, are apprehended to be very praiseworthy qualities, which deserve the esteem and approbation of every body... Carelessness and want of economy are universally disapproved of, not, however, as proceeding from a want of benevolence, but from a want

---

23 TMS, part VI, section I, ch. VI.II.4

of the proper attention to the objects of self-interest."[24]

Here Smith aligns the pursuit of private happiness with the virtue of prudence. Benevolence, he said, cannot overcome the failings of prudent concern for our own self-interest. In saying so he foreshadowed by over two centuries the contemporary debate about the importance of self-reliance for a sense of wellbeing and happiness compared with the debilitating impact of welfare dependency.

Lack of proper attention to self interest also brings to mind the concept of present bias developed by Behavioural Economists. Present bias is a high regard for now, rather than for the future. It leads to behaviour which people subsequently regret.

L Montes in *Adam Smith in Context* makes the point "Prudence is related to self-interest — It is a self-regarding virtue that fosters Smith's recurrent defence of the right of all people to the 'bettering of our condition'. The latter does not entail the cold greediness of the homo economicus as a socially detached acquisitive individual, as it demands not only the propriety of self-command, but also the approval of the impartial spectator…"[25]

The moral constraints on self-interest were also appreciated in Stoic philosophy. In this regard Cicero quotes Chrysippus the Stoic "When a man enters the foot-race, it is his duty to put forth all his strength and strive with all his might to win; but he ought never with his foot to trip, or with his hand to foul a competitor.

---

24 TMS, part VII, section I, ch. VII.II.87
25 Montes, Leonidas, 'Adam Smith in Context', p. 88

Thus in the stadium of life, it is not unfair for anyone to seek to obtain what is needful for his own advantage, but he has no right to wrest it from his neighbor."[26]

It is relevant that we have from Aristotle in *The Politics* how readily criticism of self-interest (self-love) can be misdirected: "Self-love is rightly censured, but what is really censured is not so much love of oneself as love of oneself in excess – just as we also blame the lover of money (not so much for loving money as for loving it in excess); the simple feeling of love for any of these things (self, or property, or money) is more or less universal."[27]

We are reminded here by Aristotle to focus on what is generally true, and not to generalise from exceptions. Just as there are very short and very tall people, there are extremes of human behavior, including self-interest, which at one extreme can rightly be referred to as greed and, in the worst case, as of a criminal nature.

There is also the need to take into account that the public can get a false impression from today's greatly increased media scrutiny that unscrupulous behavior is more common than is actually the case.

In *The Wealth of Nations* Smith says:

> But man has almost constant occasion for the help of his brethren, and it is in vain for him to expect it from their benevolence only. He will be more likely to prevail if he can interest their self-love (that is self-interest) in his favour and show them that it is for their own advantage to

---

26 Cicero, 'On Duties', p. 311
27 Aristotle, 'The Politics of Aristotle', p. 50

do for him what he requires of them. Whoever offers to another a bargain of any kind, proposes to do this. Give me that which I want and you shall have this that you want, is the meaning of every such offer; and it is in this manner that we obtain from one another the far greater part of those good offices which we stand in need of.[28]

He again used the metaphor of the "hidden hand" to illustrate how these transactions for mutual benefit had the unintended consequence of guiding the system towards improving living standards.

Without consciously being aware, people are involved in a multitude of transactions which are in the self-interest of both parties and mutually beneficial. Even parents exchanging days for picking up children is a case in point. Furthermore, behind these direct transactions there are multiple transactions we take for granted, required for manufacture, processing and transport of the final product. For each transaction value is added.

Smith described how manufacture of a simple item such as a woolen garment involves a great number of free market transactions. He refers to the various activities such as wool production, the shepherd and the wool-comber. Then the merchants involved, the ships employed in transport and the building of ships and so on. He explores the subject at length and concludes that the free market depends on the "co-operation of many thousands."[29]

---

28 WN, B.I, ch. 2, I.2.2
29 WN B.I, ch. 1, I.1.11

The process described by Smith is reflected today in the calculation of national production by industries undertaken by the Statistician. He calculates the value added by each industry (including the service industries) after deducting input costs that are incurred in the process of production and that involve transactions between each producer and those who supply him with goods or services used in the production process. In the case of Australian farm product, for example, in 2006-07 the value added to national production was $A22.6 billion. This was arrived at by deducting input costs of $A21.7 billion from the gross value of output of $A44.3 billion.

It is only at the margin that there are exceptions and these have been used by critics of the free market to support their case. But again it is wrong to generalise from these exceptions. They are properly considered for regulations which the community accepts as necessary and which protect the public without abandoning a free market philosophy.

For example, regulations in the pharmaceutical industry are in place to ensure product safety. Similarly, the State provides the means by which taxes, environmental standards, defence and the legal system can allow the free market to operate efficiently.

More controversial, in terms of the need for State regulation, are the recent findings of Behavioral Economists that some people have a strong bias for the present. They have difficulty overcoming habits such as problem gambling, and this requires consideration of whether government intervention is appropriate and whether such intervention introduces what Behavioral Economists see as a 'Big Brother' problem. This analysis however was not available to Smith in his time.

Smith went on to illustrate the working of self-interest in the market economy with the famous reference to customers not being able to rely on the benevolence of the butcher, the brewer or the baker for their dinner, but on their self-interest. Unfortunately critics have painted this as a picture of the customer being exploited by "self-interest".

Smith left it unstated, but had he added that neither could the butcher, the brewer or the baker have relied on the benevolence of the customer for their livelihood, then the emphasis on transactions in a free market for mutual benefit would have been apparent and consistent with the quotation above.

It follows in a competitive market that Smith would also say the butcher could not expect benevolent customers to support his livelihood if he supplied tough or contaminated meat. To be successful and "better his condition" the butcher must provide good value. Moreover, Smith would have seen the social interaction between buyer and seller as constrained by the process he analyses in *The Theory of Moral Sentiments*, which was referred to earlier.

The contemporary relevance of the importance of focus on the welfare of consumers in the market economy is emphasised by W. Edwards Deming, regarded by many as the father of modern Quality Management. He had similar thoughts about the mutual benefit of transactions when he referred to the "virtuous cycle".[30] That is, continuous market research to establish consumers' requirements and to design, manufacture and deliver products that meet those criteria.

Profit and jobs are the reward for effectively meeting consumer requirements. Loss is the penalty for failure. For example, such a penalty is now contributing to the decline of major US car companies after the long neglect of consumer requirements for a smaller fuel-efficient car.

Self-interest is therefore identified by Smith as beneficial in society and works for the advantage of all. Professor Gavin Kennedy in his authoritative book, *Adam Smith's Lost Legacy*, reaffirms the importance of self-interest: "Selfishness causes harm to others, but self-interest (not selfishness!) benefits others."[31] It is this distinction that is critical and which has been lost sight of.

The more people are encouraged to work, save, provide for their home and care for their family the more there is a benefit for others. The benefit is achieved through increased economic activity as well as a decreasing tax burden as State support is lessened.

Critics, and in particular Karl Marx, have claimed that the free market economy stands for the selfish exploitation of labour by capital. In contrast, Smith saw that in a developed economy income rewards labour and management, and rewards capital with profit for

---

30 Deming, W. Edwards, 'Out of Crisis', p. 177
31 Kennedy, Gavin, 'Adam Smith's Lost Legacy', p. 43

the risk undertaken. He says "The lowest ordinary rate of profit must always be something more than what is sufficient to compensate the occasional losses to which every employment of stock is exposed."[32]

Marx claimed all value is created by labour and therefore profit belongs to labour. The profit return to capital, Marx concluded, was expropriation by capital of what rightfully belonged to labour. This perception of exploitation was contrary to Smith's analysis of a developed free market economy and the role of profit required to encourage investment. He did say labour units could be used as a measure of value, but this was not relevant to his discussion on what was required to create value.

The perceived exploitation of labour by capital was a basic tenet on which Marx and his followers developed the case for revolution. "The expropriators are expropriated" says Marx in concluding his major work *Capital*.[33]

The outcome of pursuing Marx's philosophy was tragic – some tens of millions of people killed as victims of their own governments during the 20th century.

---

32 WN, B.I, ch. 9, I.9.18
33 Marx, Karl, 'Capital' p. 846

SELF INTEREST, SAVING, INVESTMENT AND PROSPERITY

In *The Wealth of Nations* we see self interest identified with the desire to prudently provide for the future compared with immediate consumption when Smith says "but the principle which prompts to save is the desire of bettering our condition...."[34] Moreover, Smith observes "profusion or imprudence of some being always more than compensated by the frugality and good conduct of others."[35] This supports his view that "great nations are never impoverished by private, though they are sometimes by public prodigality and misconduct."[36]

What is saved is available for investment which benefits the production of goods and services. Conversely, if investment is constrained by the availability of savings, then prosperity is adversely affected.

The following quote from *The Wealth of Nations* provides the framework of this analysis. "There is another balance, indeed, which has already been explained, very different from the balance of trade, and which, as it

34 WN, B.II, ch.3, II.3.28
35 Ibid
36 Ibid

happens to be favourable or unfavourable, necessarily occasions the prosperity or decay of every nation. This is the balance of the annual produce and consumption. If the exchangeable value of the annual produce, it has already been observed, exceeds that of the annual consumption, the capital of the society must annually increase in proportion to this excess. The society in this case lives within its revenue, and what is annually saved out of its revenue, is naturally added to its capital, and employed so as to increase still further the annual produce.

If the exchangeable value of the annual produce, on the contrary, fall short of annual consumption, the capital of the society must annually decay in proportion to this deficiency. The expense of the society in this case exceeds its revenue, and necessarily encroaches upon its capital. Its capital, therefore, must necessarily decay, and, together with it the exchangeable value of the annual produce of its industry."[37]

In addition to what Smith had to say, it is necessary to consider movements of capital (savings) to or from a country. Because of the investment opportunities, Australia has a history of net drawings on overseas savings for investment.

---

37 WN, B.IV, ch.3, IV.3.44

SELF INTEREST AND THE
BANKING SECTOR

Smith demonstrated how free competitive markets encourage buyers and sellers to reach agreements for their mutual self interest. In the light of the current financial crisis, the question needs to be asked whether self interest operates in ways that provide for mutually beneficial outcomes in the banking sector.

When people deposit money with banks, a primary concern is the security of their capital. They are looking for a safe place to keep their savings and a consideration in the form of interest payments that recognises that banks in turn will invest the deposits safely. While the modern finance industry has significantly increased in complexity, the fundamental issue raised is still relevant.

Given that bank management is investing other people's money, and when remuneration of bank management is related to fee income and profits, there is an inherent potential for what Behavioural Economists see as 'self serving bias' to increase remuneration in its various forms through taking increasing risk.

The economy is stimulated through the availability of additional credit – including to those who turn out to have little or no capacity to repay. With the passing of time, unsuspecting depositors are not aware, however, of the additional risks until it is too late. The principle of a mutually beneficial transaction between buyer and seller as discussed earlier no longer applies. Not only do depositors lose with the foreclosure of banks, but also there is downward pressure on the economy with the contraction of credit.

There is a long history of banking crises. Professor Rogoff (former Chief Economist at the IMF) has identified since 1800, thirteen banking crises in the US, twelve in the UK and eight in Germany.

In Smith's time, only three of thirty private banks in Edinburgh survived the financial crisis in Scotland in 1772.[38] He recognised the risks posed to society by banks and supported regulations to constrain their activities. He said in *The Wealth of Nations,* "Such regulations may, no doubt, be considered as in some respect a violation of natural liberty. But those exertions of the natural liberty of a few individuals, which might endanger the security of the whole society, are, and ought to be, restrained by the laws of all governments; of the most free, as well as of the most despotical. The obligation of building party walls, in order to prevent the communication of fire, is a violation of natural liberty exactly of the same kind with the regulations of the banking trade which are here proposed."[39]

---

38 Rae, John, 'The Life of Adam Smith' p.254
39 WN, B.II, ch.2, II.2.94

It seems therefore that in the 2008-2009 crisis, and in the past, Smith's 'hidden hand' has often failed to operate in the banking sector. The self interest of the depositors for security and safety of investment and the self interest of bank management are thus not automatically aligned for mutual benefit. This has led to the introduction of regulations, such as requiring banks to hold certain proportions of liabilities in capital, designed to protect depositors and the monetary system.

In the 2008-2009 world financial crisis, such regulations seem to have worked in the Australian banking industry, which appears to have remained sound despite the financial crisis. Additionally, a high standard of governance of banks would seem to have operated on this occasion.

However, similar regulations applying to the banking system overseas have clearly not been effective in preventing the crisis at the time of writing. To what extent this was due to a failure of what Smith would have regarded as governance, and an excess of selfishness, is not clear. Nor is it clear to what extent government intervention for political reasons in the banking and monetary systems have played a part. (As discussed later, government intervention in the United States directing banks to provide high risk loans for housing for the poor did aggravate the extent of the banking crisis). However, what is evident is that this part of the free market system has not operated effectively.

SMITH, THE CRITIC OF EXPLOITATION

In *The Wealth of Nations*, Smith identifies specialisation as the principal agent contributing to the generation of wealth to improve living standards. Specialisation, he goes on to say, is facilitated by free trade, capital, innovation, money, and efficient transport. All contribute to the effectiveness of specialisation in improving labour productivity, the creation of wealth and the ultimate wellbeing of the community.

In a competitive free market, respect for the needs of others is encouraged – a virtue consistent with ancient moral philosophy, namely justice – giving each his due (buyer and seller). Selfish schemes such as exploiting monopoly power, which put producers' interests ahead of the interests of consumers, debase this principle, and such schemes were the subject of the strongest possible attack by Smith.

He made a case against restrictive apprenticeships to protect guilds. He was a critic of unwarranted expansion of the role of government, which saw as being accompanied by an inclination for wasteful expenditure. He strongly criticized elements of the educational system for the self-serving behaviour of the administration and staff at the expense of students. Behavioural Economists would say this is also an example of 'self-serving bias'. He reprimanded the Church for placing opulence and luxury ahead of helping the poor. He condemned business collusion with government to gain an advantage through restrictions on trade, and he was a critic of slavery.

These were courageous and pointed attacks in 18th century Scotland. They were also astonishingly foresighted; many of Smith's arguments foreshadowed contemporary public policy debate on a number of issues such as the influence of unions and competition policy. In short, *The Wealth of Nations* was just as much a critique of exploitation and selfishness as a case promoting a free market economy.

For Smith, it was important to protect the weak and the poor against exploitation and harm. He saw government having "the duty of protecting as far as possible, every member of the society from the injustice or oppression of every other member of it..."[40] He saw the free market economy as the most effective way to create wealth and to raise the standard of living of everybody, including the working poor, a view proven by subsequent events.

---

40 WN, B.IV, ch.9, IV.9.51

THE PROPONENT OF A WELL
GOVERNED SOCIETY

Smith says in *The Wealth of Nations*:

It is the great multiplication of the productions of all the different arts, in consequence of the division of labour, which occasions, in a well-governed society, that universal opulence which extends itself to the lowest ranks of the people.[41] [And] The liberal reward of labour, therefore, as it is the necessary effect, so it is the natural symptom of increasing national wealth. The scanty maintenance of the labouring poor, on the other hand, is the natural symptom that things are at a stand, and their starving condition that they are going fast backwards.[42]

For Smith, a "well governed" society provides for free competitive markets, law and order and infrastructure. If these elements are not in place, he warns, living standards will decline and indeed in extreme cases go "fast backwards". He saw law and order as critical and if removed "... that fabric which to raise and support this

---

41 WN, B.I, ch.1, I.1.10
42 WN, B.I, ch.8, I.8.26

world … must in a moment crumble to atoms."[43] We see the wisdom of his insight, drawn from the lessons of history, when we reflect on how wages have increased and poverty has been reduced in those developing countries where there has been a freeing up of markets and the strengthening of the rule of law.

He does however qualify his views on free trade when he accepts the idea of support for establishing industries and retaliation against unfair trade practices (although he felt the latter could not be entrusted to politicians – a view of politicians perhaps unduly influenced by their behavior in his time).

As for capital, Smith saw it should move freely to where it could be most productive and benefit the community. This would suggest that takeovers which improve specialisation and therefore productivity are acceptable. On the other hand, conditions which penalise business activity may cause capital to leave a country. Takeovers purely for the purpose of increasing economic power would, however, seem outside this principle.

In many countries, the key requirements which Smith identified as necessary for improvement in living standards have often not been established by governments. The "starving condition" of the working poor, he would have observed, reflects the lack of law and order, property rights and effective government. In the extreme, we have the current case of Zimbabwe.

There has been a growing recognition of the importance Smith placed on law and order. Francis

---

43 TMS, Part II, Section I, II.II.18

Fukuyama quotes Friedman on the importance of law and order as follows: "Milton Friedman admitted that his advice to former socialist countries in the early '90s had been to "privatize, privatize, privatize". "But I was wrong," he continued, "It turns out that the rule of law is probably more basic than privatisation."[44] The rule of law would include property rights.

In relevant contemporary work Hernando de Soto in *The Mystery of Capital* demonstrates the importance of property rights for economic development. Of de Soto's work, Milton Friedman had this to say; "de Soto has demonstrated in practice that titling hitherto untitled assets is an extremely effective way to promote economic development of society as a whole. He offers politicians a project which can contribute to the welfare of their country and at the same time enhance their own political standing, a wonderful combination."[45]

---

44 *Australian Financial Review*, 4 August 2004
45 *Australian Financial Review*, 4 August 2004

THE THREAT OF GOVERNMENT INTERVENTION

The current global financial and economic crisis has raised questions about the efficacy of free markets and, in particular, the extent to which individual and corporate behaviour should be subject to government intervention and regulation to try to prevent or reduce instabilities and crises. At the same time, however, questions have also been raised as to whether government interventions have distorted the functioning of markets in ways that have contributed to, possibly even caused, the current crisis.

Experience shows that human nature has a natural tendency to swing between optimistic and pessimistic attitudes towards the outlook for the economy. Smith would have been aware of business cycles and market failures, such as the Tulip Mania in the 16th century, the South Sea Bubble of the early 18th century and the financial crisis of 1772 already mentioned. Since 1800, recurrent disruptions have been reflected in the many banking crises and recessions of varying depth, and the complexity of financial systems has increased considerably.

In assessing the adverse repercussions from the swings in the behaviour of markets, account needs to be taken of the increase in living standards to which free market policies have contributed and to the apparent capacity of countries pursuing such policies to recover strongly from any resultant reduction in economic activity. Also relevant is the relatively poor historical experience of those countries that have retained centralized economies of one form or another.

History shows that countries severely affected by these crises, but committed to free market policies, have shown strong economic performance over the longer term. The most authoritative historical analysis of economic growth is published by the OECD authored by world historical growth authority Angus Maddison in *Monitoring the World Economy 1820 – 1992.* Maddison describes the growth performance since 1820 as "dramatically superior to that in earlier history." His analysis of real per capita income growth over the period in seven groups of countries highlights the comparative success of those which have been most inclined to adopt free market policies;

Countries	Increase 1820-1992
4 Western Offshoots (USA, Canada, Australia & New Zealand)	17 fold
12 Western European Countries	13 fold
5 South European Countries	10 fold
7 Latin American Countries	7 fold
7 East European Countries	6 fold
11 Asian Countries	6 fold
10 African Countries	3 fold

Analyses of the causes of the current crisis, and of the possible implications for free market policies, range widely. However it is apparent that governments and regulators share some of the blame. The authorities responsible for regulation of the financial system in the United States and some other major countries, including central banks, evidently failed to maintain adequate control on the amount and type of credit being extended by financial intermediaries, resulting in excessive risk-taking based on unsustainable expansions of debt.

In Australia, the extent of excessive borrowing appears to have been considerably less than occurred in the USA and Europe. However, in the lead-up to 2008, the increase in the growth of monetary aggregates and household debt, coupled with the rise of inflation above the targeted range, suggests the central bank applied an insufficiently restrictive monetary policy in that period.

Further, the attitudes and actions of those authorities in advanced countries were influenced by what Smith might have described as governments' manipulation of the monetary system. This included the exertion of pressure (and in some cases legislative requirements) for financial intermediaries (some of which were owned by governments themselves) to extend credit to individuals who were not creditworthy.

Although the USA is portrayed as the leading proponent of a deregulated economic system and hence the main source of the crisis, its financial system is far from being unregulated. Nor are the financial systems of other major countries where excessive lending occurred. The situation does not appear to have been an absence of regulations, but the failure by both government and the regulatory authorities to administer those regulations, and the monetary system generally with proper regard to avoiding the creation of moral hazard situations and to maintaining stability in the financial system.

It is also apparent that the USA is far from being alone in engaging in government interventionism that influences economic behavior. European countries, for example, are running relatively high levels of general government spending (averaging well over 40% of GDP, compared with the low 30's for the USA and Australia) and their net government debt positions are also higher.

	Net Govt/Debt % GDP	Current A/C Deficit % GDP
USA	46.3	4.6
Euro Area	56.4	0.5
Japan	94.3	4.0
UK	37.6	3.6
Canada	21.5	0.9
Australia	6.3	4.9

Source: IMF World Economic Outlook 2008 (except for Australia's net debt based on ABS data).

In response to the current financial crisis, governments in a number of countries are intervening with large stimulus packages that attempt to address the decline in private expenditure during economic recession by deficit government spending. In addition, major central banks are increasing the money supply by buying corporate bond or securities. In each case there is in effect an increase in public sector debt (although central banks' liabilities in regard to the note issue or deposits by financial institutions are not shown as government debt *per se*).

A major question is whether the use of Keynesian type spending policies (as distinct from easier monetary policies which may also be in place) in a recession helps revive private investment in its role as the main driving force in the economy. Smith points out, as referred to earlier, that the "principle which prompts to save is the desire of bettering our condition" and (consistent with Keynes' much later analysis showing that saving equals investment) that "what is annually saved... is naturally added to its capital, and employed so as to increase still further the annual produce." But capital expenditure by governments can only supplement the much larger role played by private investment in modern economies (in Australia private investment is about five times larger) and the financing of public borrowings that compete with those by the private sector may inhibit the latter.

Japan's poor experience with its large increase in deficit financed public investment in the 1990s (when economic growth was only about 40 per cent of the average for advanced countries) adds weight to the view that such policies, particularly when they cause large public debt (as shown in the previous table), may not be an appropriate means of securing recovery from a recession.

When there is a significant increase in public debt, Smith warns that debasement of the currency usually follows and that states that adopt it risk being "gradually enfeebled".

He says "When national debts have once been accumulated to a certain degree, there is scarce, I believe a single instance of their having been fairly and completely paid."[46]

"The raising of the denomination of the coin has been the most usual expedient by which a real public bankruptcy has been disguised under the appearance of a pretended payment."[47]

"It occasions a general and most pernicious subversion of the fortunes of private people; enriching in most cases the idle and profuse debtor at the expense of the industrious and frugal creditor, and transporting a great part of the national capital from the hands which were likely to increase and improve it, to those which are likely to dissipate and destroy it."[48]

"Almost all states, however, ancient as well as modern, when reduced to this necessity have, upon some occasions, played this very juggling trick."[49]

As indicated, private investment is of major importance and past experience suggests that private investment may take some time. Recovery from recessionary conditions requires governments to adopt sympathetic and encouraging policies towards such investment. Roosevelt's New Deal policies to reduce unemployment and restore GDP per head to earlier levels in the US economy during the 1930s depression, appear to have been frustrated by a somewhat negative attitude by the government to big business that deterred private investment.[50]

---

46 WN, B.V, ch.3, V.3.60
47 Ibid, B.V, ch.3, V.3.61
48 Ibid, B.V, ch.3, V.3.61
49 WN, B.V, ch.3, V.3.62
50 Shlaes, Amity 'The Forgotten Man' 2007

It can be noted that real GDP per head in the USA did not recover to 1929 levels until 1940 whereas it returned to such levels by the mid 1930s in the UK and Australia. Also, the decision by the Australian Premiers to cut expenditure in 1931, acting on the advice of seven prominent economists, was subsequently praised by J M Keynes in his article published in the Melbourne Herald in June 1932.[51] This was followed by a strong growth in real GDP per head and a reduction in unemployment over the remainder of the 1930s. Consistent with Smith's warning about excessive debt levels, Keynes added that " I believe Australia has heavily over-borrowed in the past."

Following the above decision, real GDP per head increased at an average rate of 2.7% per annum to 1940.

Policies that impose costs on businesses, such as through excessive regulation, are likely to delay recovery and be inconsistent with Smith's thesis of a limited role for government.

Smith warns that over regulation can occur through the zeal of what he called "The Man of System" described as follows:

> The Man of System ... is apt to be very wise in his own conceit; and is often so enamoured with the supposed beauty of his own ideal plan of government, that he cannot suffer the smallest deviation from any part of it. He

---

51 "J.M Keynes Reviews Australia's Position, Tribute to Premiers' Plan", *Melbourne Herald*, June 1932

goes on to establish it completely, and in all its parts, without any regard either to the great interests, or to the strong prejudices which may oppose it. He seems to imagine that he can arrange the different members of a great society with as much ease as the hand arranges the different pieces upon a chess-board. He does not consider that in the great chess-board of human society, every single piece has a principle of its own, altogether different from that which the legislature might choose to impress upon it.[52]

The failure of regulatory systems in the US and other major countries to prevent a crisis can be viewed from different perspectives. On one view it might be concluded that there is a need for greatly increased regulation and fundamental changes to the structure of the financial system. Some analysts envisage that governments should even take over the operation of major financial intermediaries. The problems revealed by the operations of government controlled housing financiers, Fanny Mae and Freddie Mac, in the US, and the poor record of State banks in Australia, indicate governments are not well suited to the efficient operation of such institutions.

Alternatively, there is a question as to whether ever-increasing regulation prevents breakdowns of financial systems. The fact that Australian commercial banks were generally administered successfully leading up to the crisis suggests that effective administration of regulations is more important than the extent of regulation.

---

52 TMS, VI,VI.II.42

CONCLUSION

The world is currently questioning the role of free markets following unethical behavior and questionable or poor governance in major sectors in world financial markets. Many commentators have even called it a crisis in confidence in free markets. This has happened before, but this time it has occurred despite regulatory and monetary systems designed to prevent crises. This has called into question the efficacy of these regulations and how the regulations have been administered, including the operation of monetary policies. On past experience, however, there is no reason to suppose that free market economies will not recover from present setbacks.

It is fashionable to blame the free market for unethical behaviour and exploitation. But while critics of such behaviour can take inspiration from Smith and rightly censure the personal and moral failures of those actually responsible, including those who failed to administer regulations effectively, this does not mean the free market system itself should be blamed. Such critics should also take account of the much better records of countries that have been leaders in the pursuit of free market policies as well as the strength of their recoveries from disruptions.

Smith was not pure laissez-faire in his thinking but his basic thesis was that society needs no more than limited government. He postulated that "the sovereign has only three duties to attend to ...of great importance": national defence, the enforcement of law and order, and the establishment and maintenance of public infrastructure and institutions that would not attract profitable private investment but which would benefit society. Within these three duties, Smith envisaged the need for universal State education and regulations to protect society in relation to the operation of the banking sector.

He portrays a free market as encouraging civility through the need for mutual respect and a convergence of self-interest, between buyer and seller, for free exchange. It is a system which has been shown to raise living standards and lift millions of people out of poverty.

Smith provides an ethical framework for the free market economy based on the virtues which provide the moral case for the free exchange of goods (prudence, justice) for mutual benefit and the virtue of justice which is offended by exploitation.

In a world where moral standards are sometimes lacking and causing severe and adverse effects, he showed there is a continuing place for the virtues in setting a template or mission to guide the conduct of all participants in government and commerce.

In this context it is encouraging to note that as a result of excesses in the corporate sector there is a growing consensus to further improve ethical standards in the business sector. Increasingly companies are introducing and enforcing a Code of Conduct which provides for compliance with strict ethical standards.

ADDENDUM

DIAGRAM OF KEY FACTORS IDENTIFIED BY ADAM SMITH

The diagram on the following page shows the key elements, including self-interest, identified by Adam Smith which determine the wealth of nations. Relevant supporting references in his own words from *The Theory of Moral Sentiments* and *The Wealth of Nations* follow the diagram.

The scope of the diagram is broader than conventional economic models. In addition to identifying the causes of wealth it illustrates the factors which Smith saw as impediments to growth and the critical role of the rule of law and property rights.

The Nature and Causes of the Wealth of Nations

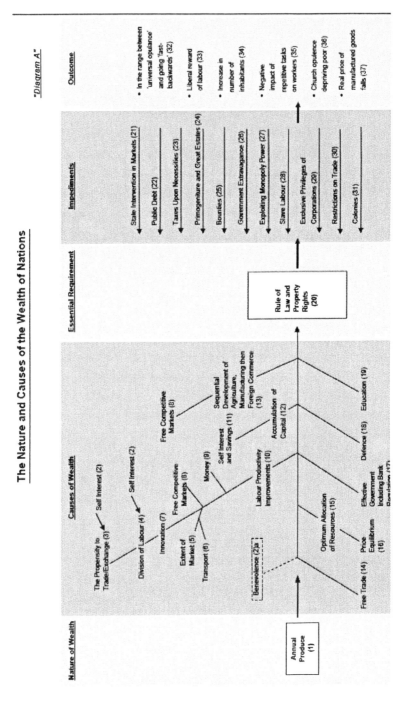

"*Diagram A*"

Nature of Wealth

Annual Produce (1)

Causes of Wealth

The Propensity to Trade/Exchange (3) → Self Interest (2)

Division of Labour (4) → Self Interest (2)

Innovation (7)

Free Competitive Markets (8)

Extent of Market (5)

Free Competitive Markets (8)

Transport (6)

Money (9)

Self Interest and Savings (11)

Sequential Development of Agriculture, Manufacturing then Foreign Commerce (13)

Labour Productivity Improvements (10)

Accumulation of Capital (12)

Benevolence (2)a

Optimum Allocation of Resources (15)

Free Trade (14)

Price Equilibrium (16)

Effective Government Including Bank Regulation (17)

Defence (18)

Education (19)

Essential Requirement

Rule of Law and Property Rights (20)

Impediments

State Intervention in Markets (21)

Public Debt (22)

Taxes Upon Necessities (23)

Primogeniture and Great Estates (24)

Bounties (25)

Government Extravagance (26)

Exploiting Monopoly Power (27)

Slave Labour (28)

Exclusive Privileges of Corporations (29)

Restrictions on Trade (30)

Colonies (31)

Outcome

- In the range between 'universal opulence' and going 'fast-backwards' (32)
- Liberal reward of labour (33)
- Increase in number of inhabitants (34)
- Negative impact of repetitive tasks on workers (35)
- Church opulence depriving poor (36)
- Real price of manufactured goods falls (37)

"AN INQUIRY INTO THE NATURE AND CAUSES OF THE WEALTH OF NATIONS"

NATURE OF WEALTH

1.   Annual Produce

"The annual labour of every nation is the fund which originally supplies it with all the necessaries and conveniences of life which it annually consumes, and which consist always either in the immediate produce of that labour, or in what is purchased with that produce from other nations."

WN, B.I, I.I.1

"The division of labour is the great cause of the increase of public opulence, which is always proportioned to the industry of the people, and not to the quantity of gold and silver as is foolishly imagined."

WN, Ed. Intro. I.15

"It would be too ridiculous to go about seriously to prove that wealth does not consist in money, or in gold and silver; but in what money purchases, and is valuable only for purchasing."

WN, B.IV, ch.1, IV.1.17

CAUSES OF WEALTH

2. Responsible for One's Self (Self Interest/Self Love)

"In every part of the universe we observe means adjusted with the nicest artifice to the ends which they are intended to produce; and in the mechanism of a plant, or animal body, admire how every thing is contrived for advancing the two great purposes of nature, the support of the individual, and the propagation of the species."

TMS, part II, II.II.19

"Every man, as the Stoics used to say, is first and principally recommended to his own care; and every man is certainly, in every respect, fitter and abler to take care of himself than of any other person."

TMS, part VI, VI.II.4

"Regard to our own private happiness and interest, too, appear upon many occasions very laudable principles of action. The habits of economy, industry, discretion, attention and application of thought are generally supposed to be cultivated from self-interested motives, and, at the same time, are apprehended to be very praiseworthy qualities, which deserve the esteem and approbation of every body ... Carelessness and want of economy are universally disapproved of, not, however, as proceeding from a want of benevolence, but from a want of the proper attention to the objects of self-interest."

TMS, part VII, VII.II.87

"The natural effort of every individual to better his own condition, when suffered to exert itself with freedom and security, is so powerful a principle, that it is alone, and without any assistance, not only capable of carrying on the society to wealth and prosperity, but of surmounting a hundred impediment and obstructions with which the folly of human laws too often encumbers its operations."

WN, Ed. Intro. I.92

2.(a)   Benevolence

"The great division of our affections is into the selfish and the benevolent."

TMS, part VII, VII.II.4

"How selfish soever man may be supposed, there are evidently some principles in his nature, which interest him in the fortune of others, and render their happiness necessary to him, though he derives nothing from it, except the pleasure of seeing it. Of this kind is pity or compassion, the emotion which we feel for the misery of others, when we either see it, or are made to conceive it in a very lively manner. That we often derive sorrow from the sorrow of others, is a matter of fact too obvious to require any instances to prove it; for this sentiment like all the other original passions of human nature, is by no means confined to the virtuous and humane, though they perhaps may feel it with the most exquisite sensibility.

The greatest ruffian, the most hardened violator of the laws of society, it is not altogether without it."

TMS, part I, I.I.1

3. The Propensity to Trade/Exchange

"Each animal is still obliged to support and defend itself, separately and independently, and derives no sort of advantage from that variety of talents with which nature has distinguished its fellows. Among men, on the contrary, the most dissimilar geniuses are of use to one another; the different produces of their respective talents, by the general disposition to truck, barter, and exchange, being brought, as it were, into a common stock, where every man may purchase whatever part of the produce of other men's talents he has occasion for."

WN, B.I, ch.2, I.2.5

"This division of labour, from which so many advantages are derived, is not originally the effect of any human wisdom, which foresees and intends that general opulence to which it gives occasion. It is the necessary, though very slow and gradual, consequence of a certain propensity in human nature which has in view no such extensive utility; the propensity to truck, barter, and exchange one thing for another."

WN, B.I, ch.2, I.2.7

"In almost every other race of animals each individual, when it is grown up to maturity, is entirely independent, and in its natural state has occasion for the assistance of no other living creature. But man has almost constant occasion for the help of his brethren, and it is in vain for him to expect it from their benevolence only. He will be more likely to prevail if he can interest their self-love in his favour, and show them that it is for their own advantage to do for him what he requires of them. Whoever offers to another a bargain of any kind, proposes to do this. Give me that which I want, and you shall have this which you want, is the meaning of every such offer; and it is in this manner that we obtain from one another the far greater part of those good offices which we stand in need of. It is not from the benevolence of the butcher, the brewer, or the baker, that we expect our dinner, but from their regard to their own interest. We address ourselves, not to their humanity but to their self-love, and never talk to them of our own necessities but of their advantages."

WN, B.I, ch.2, I.2.2

4. Division of Labour

"The greatest improvement in the productive powers of labour, and the greater part of the skill, dexterity, and judgment with which it is any where directed, or applied, seem to have been the effects of the division of labour."

WN, B.I, ch.1, I.1.1

"As it is by treaty, by barter, and by purchase, that we obtain from one another the greater part of those mutual good offices which we stand in need of, so it is this same trucking disposition which originally gives occasion to the division of labour. In a tribe of hunters or shepherds a particular person makes bows and arrows, for example, with more readiness and dexterity than any other. He frequently exchanges them for cattle or for venison with his companions; and he finds at last that he can in this manner get more cattle and venison, than if he himself went to the field to catch them. From a regard to his own interest, therefore, the making of bows and arrows grows to be his chief business, and he becomes a sort of armourer."

WN, B.I, ch.2, I.2.3

5. Extent of Market

"As it is the power of exchanging that gives occasion to the division of labour, so the extent of this division must always be limited by the extent of that power, or, in other words, by the extent of the market."

WN, B.I, ch.3, I.3.1

"By opening a new and inexhaustible market (the discovery of America) to all the commodities of Europe, it gave occasion to new divisions of labour and improvements of art, which, in the narrow circle of the ancient commerce, could never have taken place for want of a market to take off the greater part of their produce.

The productive power of labour were improved, and its produce increased in all the different countries of Europe, and together with it the real revenue and wealth of the inhabitants."

WN, B.IV, ch.1, IV.1.32

"The increase of demand, besides, though in the beginning it may sometimes raise the price of goods, never fails to lower it in the long run. It encourages production, and thereby increases the competition of the producers, who, in order to undersell one another, have recourse to new divisions of labour and new improvements of art, which might never otherwise have been thought of."

WN, B.V, ch.1, V.1.11.5

6.   Transport

"As by means of water-carriage a more extensive market is opened to every sort of industry than what land-carriage alone can afford it, so it is upon the sea-coast, and along the banks of navigable rivers, that industry of every kind naturally begins to subdivide and improve itself, and it is frequently not till a long time after that those improvements extend themselves to the inlands parts of the country."

WN, B.I, ch.3, I.3.3

"Good roads, canals, and navigable rivers, by diminishing the expense of carriage, put the remote parts of the country more nearly upon a level with those in the neighbourhood of the town. They are upon that account the greatest of all improvements. They encourage the cultivation of the remote, which must always be the most extensive circle of the country. They are advantageous to the town, by breaking down the monopoly of the country in its neighbourhood."

WN, B.I, ch.11, I.11.14

"The extent and easiness of this inland navigation was probably one of the principal causes of the early improvement of Egypt."

WN, B.I, ch.3, I.3.6

7.   Innovation

"It is naturally to be expected, therefore, that some one or other of those who are employed in each particular branch of labour should soon find out easier and readier methods of performing their own particular work, wherever the nature of it admits of such improvement. A great part of the machines made use of in those manufacturers in which labour is most subdivided, were originally the inventions of common workmen, who, being each of them employed in some simple operation, naturally turned their thoughts towards finding out easier and readier methods of performing it.

WN, B.I, ch.1, I.1.8

"I shall only observe, therefore, that the invention of all those machines by which labour is so much facilitated and abridged, seems to have been originally owing to the division of labour."

WN, B.I, ch.1, I.1.8

"All the improvements in machinery, however, have by no means been the inventions of those who had the occasion to use the machines. Many improvements have been made by the ingenuity of the makers of the machines, when to make them become the business of a particular trade; and some by that of those who are called philosophers or men of speculation, whose trade it is not to do any thing, but to observe every thing; and who, upon that account, are often capable of combining together the powers of the most distant and dissimilar objects.

In the progress of society, philosophy or speculation becomes, like every other employment, the principal or sole trade and occupation of a particular class of citizens. Like every other employment too, it is subdivided into a great number of different branches, each of which affords occupation to a particular tribe or class of philosophers; and this subdivision of employment in philosophy, as well as in every other business, improves dexterity, and saves time. Each individual becomes more expert in his own particular branch, more work is done upon the whole, and the quantity of science is considerably increased by it."

WN, B.I, ch.1, I.1.9

8.   Free Competitive Markets

"In general, if any branch of trade, or any division of labour, be advantageous to the public, the freer and more general the competition, it will always be the more so."

WN, B.I, ch.2, II.2.106

9.   Money

"The butcher has more meat in his shop than he himself can consume, and the brewer and the baker would each of them be willing to purchase a part of it. But they have nothing to offer in exchange, except the different productions of their respective trades, and the butcher is already provided with all the bread and beer, which he has immediate occasion for. No exchange can, in this case, be made between them. He cannot be their merchant, nor they his customers; and they are all of them thus mutually less serviceable to one another. In order to avoid the inconveniency of such situations, every prudent man in every period of society, after the first establishment of the division of labour, must naturally have endeavoured to manage his affairs in such a manner, as to have at all times by him, besides the peculiar produce of his own industry, a certain quantity of some one commodity or other, such as he imagined few people would be likely to refuse in exchange for the produce of their industry."

WN, B.I, ch.4, I.4.2

"In order to put industry into motion, three things are requisite; materials to work upon, tools to work with, and the wages or recompense for the sake of which the work is done. Money is neither a material to work upon, nor a tool to work with; and though the wages of the workman are commonly paid to him in money, his real revenue, like that of all other men, consists, not the money, but in the money's worth; not in the metal pieces, but in what can be got for them."

WN, B.II, ch.2, II.2.37

10. Labour Productivity Improvements

"This great increase of the quantity of work which, in consequence of the division of labour, the same number of people are capable of performing, is owing to three different circumstances; first to the increase of dexterity in every particular workman, secondly, to the saving of the time which is commonly lost in passing from one species of work to another; and lastly, to the invention of a great number of machines which facilitate and abridge labour, and enable one man to do the work of many."

WN, B.I, ch.2, I.1.5

"It is the great multiplication of the productions of all the different arts, in consequence of the division of labour, which occasions, in a well-governed society, that universal opulence which extends itself to the lowest ranks of the people."

WN, B.I, ch.1, I.1.10

11.   Self Interest and Savings

"... but the principle which prompts to save is the desire of bettering our condition..."

WN, B.II, ch.3, II.3.28

"... profusion or imprudence of some being always more than compensated by the frugality and good conduct of others."

WN, B.II, ch.3, II.3.27

"... great nations are never impoverished by private, though they are sometimes by public prodigality."

WN, B.II, ch.3, II.3.30

12.   Accumulation of Capital

"Whatever a person saves from his revenue he adds to his capital, and either employs it himself in maintaining an additional number of productive hands, or enables some other person to do so, by lending it to him for an interest, that is, for a share of the profits. As the capital of an individual can be increased only by what he saves from his annual revenue or his annual gains, so the capital of a society, which is the same with that of all the individuals who compose it, can be increased only in the same manner."

WN, B.II, ch.3, II.3.15

"As the accumulation of stock is previously necessary for carrying on this great improvement in the productive powers of labour, so that accumulation naturally leads to this improvement. The person who employs his stock in maintaining labour, necessarily wishes to employ it in such a manner as to produce as great a quantity of work as possible. He endeavours, therefore, both to make among his workmen the most proper distribution of employment, and to furnish them with the best machines which he can either invent or afford to purchase. His abilities in both these respects are generally in proportion to the extent of his stock, or to the number of people whom it can employ. The quantity of industry, therefore, not only increases in every country with the increase of the stock which employs it, but, in consequence of that increase, the same quantity of industry produces a much greater quantity of work."

WN, B.II, Intro. II.1.4

"There is another balance, indeed, which has already been explained, very different from the balance of trade and which, as it happens to be favourable or unfavourable, necessarily occasions the prosperity or decay of every nation. This is the balance of the annual produce and consumption. If the exchangeable value of the annual produce, it has already been observed, exceeds that of the annual consumption, the capital of the society must annually increase in proportion to this excess. The society in this case lives within its revenue, and what is annually saved out of its revenue, is naturally added to its capital, and employed so as to increase still further the annual produce. If the exchangeable value of the annual produce, on the contrary, fall short of annual consumption, the capital of the society must annually decay in proportion to this deficiency. The expense of the society in this case exceeds its revenue, and necessarily encroaches upon its capital. Its capital, therefore, must necessarily decay, and, together with it the exchangeable value of the annual produce of its industry."

WN, B.IV, ch.3, IV.3.44

13. Sequential Development of Agriculture, Manufacturing then Foreign Commerce

"According to the natural course of things, therefore, the greater part of the capital of every growing society is, first, directed to agriculture, afterwards to manufactures, and last of all to foreign commerce. This order of things is so very natural, that in every society that had any territory, it has always, I believe, been in some degree observed. Some of their lands must have been cultivated before any considerable towns could be established, and some sort of coarse industry of the manufacturing kind must have been carried on in those towns, before they could well think of employing themselves in foreign commerce."

WN, B.III, ch.1, III.1.8

14. Free Trade

"The love of our own nation often disposes us to view, with the most malignant jealousy and envy, the prosperity and aggrandisement of any other neighbouring nation. Independent and neighbouring nations, having no common superior to decide their disputes, all live in continual dread and suspicion of one another. Each sovereign, expecting little justice from his neighbours, is disposed to treat them with as little as he expects from them. The regard for the laws of nations, or for those rules which independent states profess or pretend to think themselves bound to observe in their dealings with one another, is often very little more than mere pretence and profession. From the smallest interest, upon the slightest provocation, we see those rules every day either evaded or directly violated without shame or remorse. Each nation foresees, or imagines it foresees, its own subjugation in the increasing power and aggrandisement of any of its neighbours; and the mean principle of national prejudice is often founded on the noble one of the love of our own country. France and England may each of them have some reason to dread the increase of the naval and military power of the other; but for either of them to envy the internal happiness and prosperity of the other, the cultivation of its lands, the advancement of its manufacturers, the increase of its commerce, the security and number of its ports and harbours, its proficiency in all the liberal arts and sciences, is surely beneath the dignity of two such great nations. These are the real improvements of the world we live in. Mankind are benefited, human nature is ennobled by them. In such improvements each nations ought not only to endeavour itself to excel, but, from the love of mankind, to promote, instead of obstructing, the excellence of its neighbours. These are all proper objects of national emulation, not of national prejudice or envy."

TMS, part VI, VI.11.28

"The importation of gold and silver is not the principal, much less the sole benefit which a nation derives from its foreign trade. Between whatever places foreign trade is carried on, they all of them drive two distinct benefits from it. It carries out that surplus part of the produce of their land and labour for which there is no demand among them, and brings back in returns for it something else which there is a demand. It gives a value to their superfluities, by exchanging them for something else, which may satisfy a part of their wants, and increase their enjoyments. By means of it, the narrowness of the home market does not hinder the division of labour in any particular branch of art or manufacture from being carried to the highest perfection. By opening a more extensive market for whatever part of the produce of their labour may exceed the home consumption, it encourages them to improve its productive powers, and to augment its annual produce to the utmost, and thereby to increase the real revenue and wealth of the society."

WN, B.IV, ch.1, IV.1.31

"What is prudence in the conduct of every private family, can scarce be folly in that of a great kingdom. If a foreign country can supply us with a commodity cheaper than we ourselves can make it, better buy it of them with some part of the produce of our own industry, employed in a way in which we have some advantage."

WN, B.IV, ch.2, IV.2.12

"Were all nations to follow the liberal system of free exportation and free importation, the different states into which a great continent was divided would so far resemble the different provinces of a great empire."

WN, B.IV, ch.5, IV.5.78

"The case in which it may sometimes be a matter of deliberation, how far, or in what manner, it is proper to restore the free importation of foreign goods, after it has been for some time interrupted, is, when particular manufacturers, by means of high duties or prohibitions upon all foreign goods which can come into competition with them, have been so far extended as to employ a great multitude of hands. Humanity may in this case require that the freedom of trade should be restored only by slow gradations, and with a good deal of reserve and circumspection. Were those high duties and prohibitions taken away all at once, cheaper foreign goods of the same kind might be poured so fast into the home market, as to deprive all at once many thousands of our people of their ordinary employment and means of subsistence."[a]

WN, B.IV, ch.2, IV.2.38

"If any particular manufacture was necessary, indeed, for the defence of the society, it might not always be prudent to depend on our neighbors for the supply; and if manufacture could not otherwise be supported at home, it might be not be unreasonable that all the other branches of industry should be taxed in order to support it."

WN, B.IV, ch.5, IV.5.36

"According to this liberal and generous system, therefore, the most advantageous method in which a landed nation can rise up artificers, manufacturers and merchants of its own, is to grant the most perfect freedom of trade to the artificers, manufactures and merchants of all other nations. It thereby raises the value of the surplus produce of its own land, of which the continual increase gradually establishes a fund, which in due time necessarily raises up all the artificers, manufacturers and merchants whom it has occasion for.

WN, B.14, ch.9, IV.9.24

15.   Optimum Allocation of Resources

"The whole of the advantages and disadvantages of the different employments of labour and stock must, in the same neighbourhood, be either perfectly equal or continually tending to equality. If in the same neighbourhood, there was any employment evidently either more or less advantageous than the rest, so many people would crowd into it in the one case, and so many would desert it in the other, that its advantages would soon return to the level of other employments. This at least would be the case in a society where things were left to follow their natural course, where there is perfect liberty, and where every man was perfectly free both to choose what occupation be thought proper, and to change it as often as he thought proper. Every man's interest would prompt him to seek the advantageous, and to shun the disadvantageous employment.

Every individual is continually exerting himself to find out the most advantageous employment for whatever capital he can command. It is his own advantage, indeed, and not that of the society which he has in view. But the study of his own advantage naturally, or rather necessarily leads him to prefer that employment which is most advantageous to the society."

WN, B.I, ch.10, I.10.1

16.　Price Equilibrium

"When the price of any commodity is neither more nor less than what is sufficient to pay the rent of the land, the wages of the labour, and the profits of the stock employed in raising, preparing, and bringing it to market, according to their natural rates, the commodity is then sold for what may be called its natural price."

WN, B.I, ch.7, I.7.4

"The actual price at which any commodity is commonly sold is called its market price. It may either be above, or below, or exactly the same with its natural price."

WN, B.I, ch.7, I.7.7

17.   Effective Government and Banking

"According to the system of natural liberty, the sovereign has only three duties to attend to; three duties of great importance, indeed, but plain and intelligible to common understandings: first, the duty of protecting the society from the violence and invasion of other independent societies; secondly, the duty of protecting as far as possible, every member of the society from the injustice or oppression of every other member of it, or the duty of establishing an exact administration of justice; and, thirdly, the duty of erecting and maintaining certain public works and certain public institutions which it can never be for the interest of any individual, or small number of individuals, to erect and maintain, because the profit could never repay the expense to any individual or small number of individuals, though it may frequently do much more than repay it to a great society."

WN, B.IV, ch.9, IV.9.51

He recognised the risks posed to society by banks and supported regulations to constrain their activities. "Such regulations may, no doubt, be considered as in some respect a violation of natural liberty. But those exertions of the natural liberty of a few individuals, which might endanger the security of the whole society, are, and ought to be, restrained by the laws of all governments; of the most free, as well as of the most despotical. The obligation of building party walls, in order to prevent the communication of fire, is a violation of natural liberty, exactly of the same kind with the regulations of the banking trade which are here proposed."

WN, B.II, ch.2, II.2.94

18.   Defence

"The first duty of the sovereign, that of protecting the society from the violence and invasion of other independent societies, can be performed only by means of a military force. But the expense both of preparing this military force in time of peace, and of employing it in time of war, is very different in the different states of society, in the different periods of improvement.

WN, B.V, ch.1, V.1.0

"An industrious, and upon that account wealthy nation, is of all nations the most likely to be attacked; and unless the state takes some new measures for the public defence, the natural habits of the people render them altogether incapable of defending themselves."

WN, B.V, ch.1, V.1.14

19.   Education

"But though the common people cannot, in any civilized society, be so well instructed as people of some rank and fortune, the most essential parts of education, however, to read, write, and account, can be acquired at so early a period of life, that the greater part even of those who are to be bred to the lowest occupations, have time to acquire them before they can be employed in those occupations.

For a very small expense the public can facilitate, can encourage, and can even impose upon almost the whole body of the people, the necessity of acquiring those most essential parts of education."

WN, B.V, ch.1, V.1.182

(Of the four items of fixed capital of society) – "... the acquired and useful abilities of all the inhabitants or members of the society. The acquisition of such talents, by the maintenance of the acquirer during his education, study, or apprenticeship, always costs a real expense, which is a capital fixed and realized, as it were, in his person. Those talents, as they make a part of his fortune, so do they likewise of that of the society to which he belongs. The improved dexterity of a workman may be considered in the same light as a machine or instrument of trade which facilitates and abridges labour, and which, although it costs a certain expense, repays that expense with a profit."

WN, B.II, ch.1, II.1.17

ESSENTIAL REQUIREMENTS

20. Rule of Law and Property Rights

"Justice, on the contrary, is the main pillar that upholds the noble edifice. If it is removed, the great, the immense fabric of human society, that fabric which to raise and support in this world if I may say so has the peculiar and darling care of Nature, must in a moment crumble into atoms."

TMS, part II, II.II.18

"If there is any society among robbers and murderers, they must at least, according to the trite observation, abstain from robbing and murdering one another. Beneficence, therefore, is less essential to the existence of society than justice. Society may subsist, though not in the most comfortable state, without beneficence; but the prevalence of injustice must utterly destroy it.

TMS, part II, II.II.17

"The acquisition of valuable and extensive property, therefore, necessarily requires the establishment of civil government."

WN, B.V, ch.1, V.1.45

"Commerce and manufactures can seldom flourish long in any state which does not enjoy a regular administration of justice, in which the people do not feel themselves secure in the possession of their property, in which the faith of contracts is not supported to be regularly employed in enforcing the payment of debts from all those who are able to pay. Commerce and manufactures, in short, can seldom flourish in any state in which there is not a certain degree of confidence in the justice of government."

WN, B.V, ch.3, V.3.7

IMPEDIMENTS

21.   State Intervention in the Market

"What is the species of domestic industry which his capital can employ, and of which the produce is likely to be of the greatest value, every individual, it is evident, can in his local situation, judge much better than any statesman or lawgiver can do for him. The statesman, who should attempt to direct private people in what manner they ought to employ their capitals, would not only load himself with a most unnecessary attention, but assume an authority which could safely be trusted, not only to no single person, but to no council or senate whatever, and which would no-where be so dangerous as in the hands of a man who had folly and presumption enough to fancy himself fit to exercise it."

WN, B.IV, ch.2, IV.2.10

"Consumption is the sole end and purpose of all production; and the interest of the producer ought to be attended to, only so far as it may be necessary for promoting that of the consumer. The maxim is so perfectly self-evident, that it would be absurd to attempt to prove it. But in the mercantile system, the interest of the consumer is almost constantly sacrificed to that of the producer; and it seems to consider production, and not consumption, as the ultimate end and object of all industry and commerce."

WN, B.IV, ch.8, IV.8.49

"It cannot be very difficult to determine who have been the contrivers of this whole mercantile system; not the consumers, we may believe, whose interest has been entirely neglected; but the producers, whose interest has so carefully been attended to; and among this latter class our merchants and manufacturers have been by far the principal architects. In the mercantile regulations … the interest of our manufacturers has been most peculiarly attended to; and the interest, not so much of the consumers, as that of some other sets of producers, has been sacrificed to it.

WN, B.IV, ch.8, IV.8.54

"It is thus that every system which endeavours, either, by extraordinary encouragements, to draw towards a particular species of industry a greater share of the capital of the society than what would naturally go to it; or by extraordinary restraints, to force from a particular species of industry some share of the capital which would otherwise be employed in it; is in reality subversive of the great purpose which it means to promote. It retards, instead of accelerating; the progress of the society towards real wealth and greatness; and diminishes, instead of increasing, the real value of the annual produce of its land and labour."

WN, B.IV, ch.9, IV.9.50

"That indolence, which is the natural effect of the ease and security of their situation, renders them too often, not only ignorant, but incapable of that application of mind which is necessary in order to foresee and understand the consequences of any public regulation."

WN, B.I, ch.11, I.11.262

"The Man of System ... is apt to be very wise in his own conceit; and is often so enamoured with the supposed beauty of his own ideal plan of government, that he cannot suffer the smallest deviation from any part of it. He goes on to establish it completely, and in all its parts, without any regard either to the great interests, or to the strong prejudices which may oppose it. He seems to imagine that he can arrange the different members of a great society with as much ease as the hand arranges the different pieces upon a chess-board. He does not consider that in the great chess-board of human society, every single piece has a principle of its own, altogether different from that which the legislature might choose to impress upon it."[b]

22.   Public Debt

"The practice of funding has gradually enfeebled every state which has adopted it. The Italian republics seem to have begun it. Genoa and Venice, the only two remaining which can pretend to an independent existence, have both been enfeebled by it. Spain seems to have learned the practice from the Italian republics, and (its taxes being probably less judicious than theirs) it has, in proportion to its natural strength, been still more enfeebled. The debts of Spain are of very old standing. It was deeply in debt before the end of the sixteenth century, about a hundred years before England owed a shilling. France, notwithstanding all its natural resources, languishes under an oppressive load of the same kind. The republic of the United Provinces is as much enfeebled by its debts as either Genoa and Venice."

WN, B.V, ch.3, V.3.58

23.   Taxes Upon Necessities

"In Holland the heavy taxes upon the necessaries of life have ruined, it is said, their principal manufactures, and are likely to discourage gradually even their fisheries and their trade in ship-building. The taxes upon the necessaries of life are inconsiderable in Great Britain, and no manufacture has hitherto been ruined by them."

WN, B.V, ch.2, V.2.224

24.   Primogeniture and Great Estates

"Great tracts of uncultivated land were, in this manner not only engrossed by particular families, but the possibility of their being divided again was as much as possible precluded for ever. It seldom happens, however, that a great proprietor is a great improver. In the disorderly times which gave birth to those barbarous institutions, the great proprietor was sufficiently employed in defending his own territories, or in extending his jurisdiction and authority over those of his neighbours. He had no leisure to attend to the cultivation and improvement of land. When the establishment of law and order afforded him this leisure, he often wanted the inclination, and almost always the requisite abilities. If the expense of his house and person either equaled or exceeded his revenue, as it did very frequently, he had no stock to employ in this manner. If he was an economist, he generally found it more profitable to employ his annual savings in new purchases, than in the improvement of his old estate. To improve land with profit, like all other commercial projects, requires an exact attention to small savings and small gains, of which a man born to a great fortune, even though naturally frugal, is very seldom capable. The situation of such a person naturally disposes him to attend rather than ornament which pleases his fancy, than to profit for which he has so little occasion. The elegance of his dress, of his equipage, of his house, and household furniture, are objects which from his infancy he has been accustomed to have some anxiety about. The turn of mind which this habit naturally forms, follows him when he comes to think of the improvement of land. He embellishes perhaps four or five hundred acres in the neighbourhood of his house, at ten times the expense which the land is worth after all his improvements; and finds that if he was to improve his whole estate in the same manner and he has little taste for any other, he would be a bankrupt before he had finished the tenth part of it. There still remain in both parts of the United Kingdom some great estates which have continued without interruption in the hands of the same family since the times of feudal anarchy. Compare the present condition of these estates with the possessions of the small proprietors in their neighbourhood and you will require no other argument to convince you how unfavourable such extensive property is to improvement."

WN, B.III, ch.2, III.2.7

25. Bounties

"The effect of bounties, like that of all the other expedients of the mercantile system, can only be to force the trade of a country into a channel much less advantageous than that in which it would naturally run of its own accord."

WN, B.IV, ch.5, IV.5.3

"The laws concerning corn may every where be compared to the laws concerning religion. The people feel themselves so much interested in what relates either to their subsistence in this life, or to their happiness in a life to come, that government must yield to their prejudices, and, in order to preserve the public tranquility, establish that system which they approve of. It is upon this account, perhaps, that we so seldom find a reasonable system established with regard to either of those two capital objects."

WN, B.IV, ch.5, IV.5.79

"… the bounty to the white herring fishery is a tonnage bounty; and is proportioned to the burden of the ship, not to her diligence or success in the fishery; and it has, I am afraid, been too common for vessels to fit out for the sole purpose of catching, not the fish, but the bounty."

WN, B.IV, ch.5, IV.5.32

26.   Government Extravagance

"It is of the highest impertinence and presumption, therefore, in kings and ministers, to pretend to watch over the economy of private people, and to restrain their expense, either by sumptuary laws, or by prohibiting the importation of foreign luxuries. They are themselves always, and without any exception, the greatest spendthrifts in the society. Let them look well after their own expense, and they may safely trust private people with theirs. If their own extravagance does not ruin the state, that of their subjects never will."

WN, B.II, ch.3, II.3.36

27. Exploiting Monopoly Power

"A monopoly granted either to an individual or to a trading company has the same effect as a secret in trade or manufactures. The monopolists, by keeping the market constantly under-stocked, by never fully supplying the effectual demand, sell their commodities much above the natural price, and raise their emoluments whether they consist in wages or profit, greatly above their natural rate."

WN, B.I, ch.7, I.7.26

"People of the same trade seldom meet together, even for merriment and diversion, but the conversation ends in a conspiracy against the public, or in some contrivance to raise prices. It is impossible indeed to prevent such meetings, by any law which either could be executed, or would be consistent with liberty and justice. But though the law cannot hinder people of the same trade from sometimes assembling together, it ought to do nothing to facilitate such assemblies, much less to render than necessary."

WN, B.I, ch.10, I.10.82

"The single advantage which the monopoly procures to a single order of men is in many different ways hurtful to the general interest of the country."

WN, B.IV, ch.7, IV.7.148

"…. To attempt to diminish in any respect the monopoly which our manufacturers have obtained against us. This monopoly has so much increased the number of some particular tribes of them, that, like an overgrown standing army, they have become formidable to the government, and upon many occasions intimidate the legislature. The member of parliament who supports every proposal for strengthening this monopoly, is sure to acquire not only the reputation of understanding trade, but great popularity and influence with an order of men whose numbers and wealth render them of great importance. If he opposes them, on the contrary, and still more if he has authority enough to be able to thwart them, neither the most acknowledged probity, nor the highest rank, nor the greatest public services, can protect him from the most infamous abuse and detraction, from personal insults, nor sometimes from real danger, arising from the insolent outrage of furious and disappointed monopolists."

WN, B.IV, ch.2, IV.2.43

28. Slave Labour

"It appears, accordingly, from the experience of all ages and nations, I believe, that the work done by freemen comes cheaper in the end that that performed by slaves…"

WN, B.I, ch.8, I.8.40

"The liberal reward of labour, therefore, as it is the effect of increasing wealth, so it is the cause of increasing population. To complain of it is to lament over the necessary effect and cause of the greatest public prosperity."

WN, B.I, ch.8, I.8.41

"But if great improvements are seldom to be expected from great proprietors, they are least of all to be expected when they employ slaves for their workmen. The experience of all ages and nations, I believe, demonstrates that the work done by slaves, though it appears to cost only their maintenance, is in the end the dearest of any. A person who can acquire no property, can have no other interest but to eat as much, and to labour as little as possible."

WN, B.III, ch.2, III.2.9

29.   Exclusive Privileges of Corporations

"The constant view of such companies is always to raise the rate of their own profit as high as they can; to keep the market, both for the goods which they export, and for those which they import, as much under stocked as they can: which can be done only by restraining the competition, or by discouraging new adventurers from entering the trade."

WN, B.V, ch.1, V.1.99

30.   Restrictions on Trade

"By means of glasses, hotbeds, and hotwalls, very good grapes can be raised in Scotland, and very good wine too can be made of them at about thirty times the expense for which at least equally good can be brought from foreign countries. Would it be a reasonable law to prohibit the importation of all foreign wines, merely to encourage the making of claret and burgundy in Scotland?"

WN, B.IV, ch.2, IV.2.15

31.   Colonies

"After all the unjust attempts, therefore, of every country in Europe to engross to itself the whole advantage of the trade of its own colonies, no country has yet been able to engross to itself any thing but the expense of supporting in time of peace and of defending in time of war the oppressive authority which it assumes over them. The inconveniences resulting from the possession of its colonies, every country has engrossed to itself completely. The advantages resulting from their trade it has been obliged to share with many other countries."

WN, B.IV, ch.7, IV.7.170

"Great Britain derives nothing but loss from the dominion which she assumes over her colonies."

WN, B.IV, ch.7, IV.7.151

OUTCOME

32. In the range between "universal opulence" and "going fast backwards"

"It is the great multiplication of the productions of all the different arts, in consequence of the division of labour, which occasions, in a well-governed society, that universal opulence which extends itself to the lowest ranks of the people."

WN, B.I, ch.1, I.10.10

"The liberal reward of labour, therefore, as it is the necessary effect, so it is the natural symptom of increasing national wealth. The scanty maintenance of the labouring poor, on the other hand, is the natural symptom that things are at a stand, and their starving condition that they are going fast backwards."

WN, B.I, ch.8, I.8.26

33. Liberal Reward of Labour

"It is the great multiplication of the productions of all the different arts, in consequence of the division of labour, which occasions, in a well-governed society, that universal opulence which extends itself to the lowest ranks of the people.

WN, B.I, ch.1, I.10.10

The liberal reward of labour, therefore, as it is the necessary effect, so it is the natural symptom of increasing national wealth."

WN, B.I, ch.8, I.8.26

34.   Increase in Number of Inhabitants

"The liberal reward of labour, therefore, as it is the effect of increasing wealth, so it is the cause of increasing population.   To complain of it, is to lament over the necessary effect and cause of the greatest public prosperity."

WN, B.I, ch.8, I.8.41

35.   Negative Impact of Repetitive Tasks on Workers

"It is the progress of the division to of labour, the employment of the far greater part of those who live by labour, that is, of the great body of the people, comes to be confined to a few very simple operations; frequently to one or two.   But the understandings of the greater part of men are necessarily formed by their ordinary employments.   The man whose whole life is spent in performing a few simple operations, of which the effects too are, perhaps, always the same, or very nearly the same, has no occasion to exert his understanding, or to exercise his invention in finding out expedients for removing difficulties which never occur.   He naturally loses, therefore, the habit of such exertion, and generally becomes as stupid and ignorant as it is possible for a human creature to become. The torpor of his mind renders him, not only incapable of relishing or bearing a part in any national conversation, but of conceiving any generous, noble, or tender sentiment, and consequently of forming any just judgment concerning many even of the ordinary duties of private life. Of the great and extensive interests of his country he is altogether incapable of judging; and unless very particular pains have been taken to render him otherwise, he is equally incapable of defending his country in war. The uniformity of his stationary life naturally corrupts the courage of his mind, and makes him regard with abhorrence the irregular, uncertain, and adventurous life of a soldier. It corrupts even the activity of his body, and renders him incapable of exerting his strength with vigor and perseverance, in any other employment than that to which he has been bred. His dexterity at his own particular trade seems, in this manner, to be acquired at the expense of his intellectual, social, and martial virtues. But in every improved and civilized society this is the state into which the labouring poor, that is, the great body of the people, must necessarily fall, unless government take some pains to prevent it."

WN, B.V, ch.1, V.1.178

36.   Church Opulence Depriving Poor

"In the produce of arts, manufactures, and commerce, the clergy, like the great barons, found something for which they could exchange their rude produce, and thereby discovered the means of spending their whole revenues upon their own persons, without giving any considerable share of them to other people.   Their charity became gradually less extensive, their hospitality less liberal or less profuse.

The inferior ranks of people no longer looked upon that order, as they had done before, as the comforters of their distress, and the relievers of their indigence. On the contrary, they were provoked and disgusted by the vanity, luxury, and expense of the richer clergy, who appeared to spend upon their own pleasures what had always before been regarded as the patrimony of the poor."

WN, B.V, ch.1, V.1.214

37.   Decline in Price of Manufactured Goods

"It is the natural effect of improvement, however, to diminish gradually the real price of almost all manufactures."

WN, B.I, ch.11, I.11.216

ENDNOTES

a Smith does say however that the effect would be "much less than is commonly imagined" for two reasons. Firstly, employment in export industries would not be effected and secondly the people thrown out of work may readily find alternative employment.

b There is a nice example of the accuracy of Smith's insight into the mind of the "Man of System" related in "The Closed Circle" by David Pryce-Jones. It is a record of Muhammad Ali, the ruler of Egypt from 1811 to 1849, speaking to the British Consul in 1826.

> "I collected all power into my hands in order to ensure efficiency. The question is one concerned with production, and if I fail to act, who else would? Who is going to provide the necessary funds, suggest the plans to be followed and the crops to be planted? Who is going to force the people to acquire knowledge and sciences which made Europe progress? I was forced to lead this country as children must be led because allowing it to function alone would only lead to chaos again."

A contemporary witness describes how Muhummad Ali and his state "inflicted terrible or harsh duties on women of poor areas, subjecting them to forced labour which the entire population of several villages, men, women, children and young girls, led by the sheikh al-balad (a man designated to be mayor), were taken, chained, and laboriously found their way to the appointed place. They were forced to buy cloth of the state at a price fixed by the administration and were forbidden to weave their own clothes. All dresses had to bear a stamp attesting that the material came from government stores.

REFERENCES

Aristotle. *The Politics of Aristotle Edited and Translated by Ernest Barker* Oxford University Press 1958.

Cicero. 2005. On Duties. Loeb Classical Library.

Coleman, William Dr. *Economics and its Enemies.*

Deming, Edwards W. 1998 *Out of Crisis.* Massachusetts Institute of Technology.

The Theory of Moral Sentiments Adam Smith. Edited by D. D. Raphael and A. L. Macfie. 1976. Oxford University Press.

The Wealth of Nations Adam Smith Vol 1 & 2. Edited by Edwin Cannan. 1961. Butler and Tanner Ltd.

Fehr, Ernst. *Simon Gachter, The Journal of Economic Perspectives.*

Kennedy, Gavin. 2005. *Adam Smith's Lost Legacy.* Palgrave Macmillan

J M Keynes Reviews Australia's Position, Tribute to Premiers' Plan" Melbourne Herald, June 1932

Marx, Karl. 1974. Capital J. M. Dent & Sons Ltd.

Maddison, Angus. Monitoring *The World Economy, 1820 – 1992* Development Centre Studies OECD Paris 1995.

Montes, Leonidas. 2004. *Adam Smith in Context – A Critical Reassessment of some Central Components of His Thought.* Palgrave Macmillan

Murdoch, Iris. *The Sovereignty of Good Over Other Concepts.*

Rae, John. 2006. *The Life of Adam Smith.* Cosimo Inc.

Shlaes, Amity. *2007 'The Forgotten Man', Harper Collins Publishers, New York.*

Skousen, Mark. *The Making of Modern Economics* M E Sharpe Inc. 2001

Stewart, Dugald. 1793. *Account of the Life and Writings of Adam Smith.* Transactions of the Royal Society of Edinburgh.

ABOUT THE AUTHOR

Richard Morgan AM is Chairman of BPC Holdings Pty Limited, a private company with interests in Australian agri-business and venture capital. He had a career in industry and was most recently General Manager of the Fertilizer Division of WMC Limited, Deputy Chairman of WMC Fertilizer Limited and Chairman of Hi Fert Pty Limited.

He has served as a Director and Treasurer of the Victorian Chamber of Commerce and Industry. He was a Council Member and National Treasurer of the Australian Institute of Agriculture Science and Technology and was made a Fellow of the Institute for his contribution to the Australian Fertilizer Industry. He served as Council Member of Geelong Grammar School and the Australia Institute of International Affairs Victorian Branch. He has also been past National Chairman of the Australian Red Cross Society and a member of The Australian Red Cross Blood Service Board. He has degrees in Agricultural Science and Commerce and has been a tutor of Economics at The Faculty of Economics and Commerce, The University of Melbourne.